MELT 2 MOULD

Profitable Plastic Secrets nobody will tell you

MELT 2 MOULD

Profitable Plastic Secrets nobody will tell you

PARVEEN SHARMA

Worldwide Published by

Pendown Press

PENDOWN PRESS LLP

An ISO 9001 & ISO 14001 Certified Co.,

Regd. Office: 3767A, Kanhaiya Nagar,

Tri Nagar, Delhi-110035

Ph.: 8130886000, 9650072927, 8595249536

E-mail: info@pendownpress.com

Branch Office: 1A/2A, 20, Hari Sadan, Ansari Road,

Daryaganj, New Delhi-110002

Ph.: 011-45794768

Website: PendownPress.com

First Edition: 2024

Price: ₹499/-

ISBN: 978-93-5554-929-7

Layout and Cover Designed by Pendown Graphics Team

Printed and Bound in India by Thomson Press India Ltd.

Dedication

As I sit down to pen the opening words of this book, a flood of memories washes over me — memories of a man whose unwavering support, profound wisdom, and enduring love laid the foundation for everything that I am today. My beloved father, Punam Chand Sharma, who left us on a winter day, December 28, 2023.

On that December day, when the world bade you farewell, a piece of my heart melted away with you. Yet, just as plastics transform from a malleable state to a structured form, so too have the lessons you imparted molded me into the person I am today. You were my anchor in the storm, a steady force that shaped the contours of my character.

Papa, you were the one who first sparked my curiosity in the world of science and innovation. Your workshop, filled with the hum of machines and the fabrication work of sheet metal, was my first classroom. You taught me the art of making the machines — not just for plastics but ideas, dreams, and aspirations.

As a child, I found your workbench to be a world of endless possibilities, where I marveled at the magical transformation of Raw Materials into Machines that combined utility and beauty. Unaware at the time, these initial impressions evolved into a deep fascination, guiding my journey in ways I could never have anticipated.

This book is a tribute to your memory, a chronicle of my journey that carries the echoes of your voice, the warmth of your encouragement, and the resilient spirit that you instilled in me. Through each word on these pages, I hope to honor the legacy you left behind, not just as a father but as a guiding light that continues to illuminate my path.

In this exploration of "Melt to Mold," I dedicate every insight, every discovery, and every moment of clarity to you. Your presence is felt in every chapter, a silent mentor guiding the way. Though the physical realm may keep us apart, your wisdom lives on, moulding the very fabric of my existence.

With each page, may your spirit resonate, connecting memories with the present. In this journey of making plastic processing machines, I find comfort in knowing your impact, like plastic, is enduring and everlasting.

In loving memory of my dearest father, who taught me that even in the melting moments of life, we can find the strength to mold a legacy that withstands the test of time.

Forever in my heart, Your Son

Parveen Sharma

Contents

The Journey of Parveen Sharma and
Hinds Plastic Machines Pvt. Ltd.   i
Introduction   v
Who Will Benefit   vi
Book Perspective   vii

Chapter 01

Understanding Plastic Processing   1

Chapter 02

Polymer Preparation   4

Chapter 03

Plastic Processing Methods   10

Chapter 04

Moulds and Dies   19

Chapter 05

Process Optimization   33

Chapter 06
Quality Control   44

Chapter 07
Post-processing and Finishing   48

Chapter 08
Case Studies   53

Chapter 09
Future of Plastic Processing   66

Chapter 10
Conclusion   72

The Journey of Parveen Sharma and Hinds Plastic Machines Pvt. Ltd.

Hello, I am Parveen Sharma, a mechanical engineer by profession and the Managing Director of Hinds Plastic Machines Pvt. Ltd. My journey an engineering began at CRSCE Murthal, now known as DCRUST, where my passion for engineering and innovation took root.

From a young age, I was deeply fascinated by engineering. This passion was reflected in my childhood toys, many of which I crafted myself in my father's workshop. I remember creating a cricket stamp from an MS pipe in eighth grade and fashioning a spinning toy out of aluminium on a lathe machine. My entire childhood was an exploration of engineering, a journey marked by my achievements as a topper in Engineering Drawing in the CBSE Board and during my college years.

In my final year of B.Tech, I undertook a major project where I developed an Angular Wheel and V Groove Slide System, an innovative design that eliminated the need for a differential axle. After completing my degree, I built a Hydraulic Press Brake for my father's small sheet metal fabrication workshop, marking the beginning of my professional journey in machine manufacturing.

In 1998, I joined Joy Dzign Engineer in Delhi as a Design and Development Engineer. This role introduced me to the world of small plunger-type vertical injection moulding machines. It was here that I recognized the growing demand for high-quality, efficient, and sustainable plastic processing machine manufacturing solutions. Seeing an opportunity to make a significant impact in the plastic industry, I founded Hinds Machineries in 1999, focusing on manufacturing plastic processing machines ranging from 50 to 450 tons clamping force.

A major milestone came in 2003 when I launched the first Euro Series Injection Moulding Machine at PlastIndia 2003 in Pragati Maidan, New Delhi. The overwhelming response at PlastIndia propelled our expansion to a 450 sqm factory in Haryana IMT Manesar. As demand continued to rise across India, we further expanded with another unit in Sector 8, IMT Manesar, opposite Maruti gate no. 2, and rebranded to Hinds Plastic Machines Pvt. Ltd.

Our contribution to the Make in India program has been significant. A notable instance during the COVID-19 pandemic highlighted our commitment to innovation and customer service. One of our clients, who is in the manufacturing of medical Endotracheal tubes, faced a challenging situation when a Chinese blow moulding machine, which they had purchased, failed to start after the lockdown.

Despite their efforts, including procuring a new microprocessor from China, the machine remained non-functional. When they reached out to me, I was able to replace the microprocessor and get the machine running within two days. This experience led to the development of the first Indian Blow Moulding machine for ETT Cuffs manufacture, a product that proved to be faster, more reliable, and more energy-efficient than its Chinese counterparts.

As we celebrate our silver jubilee, we are excited to announce the launch of an advanced and innovative All-Electric Blow Moulding machine for ETT Cuffs manufacture in India. This marks another milestone for Hinds Plastic Machines Pvt. Ltd. as we continue to innovate and lead in the plastic machinery sector.

I am also proud to share that our machines have contributed to national achievements, including the development of parts through our machine, used by ISRO in the launch of Chandrayaan-3.

This journey, from a curious child in a workshop to the Managing Director of a leading machine manufacturing company, has been a testament to the power of innovation and the relentless pursuit of engineering excellence.

Introduction

Welcome to *"Melt to Mold: A Comprehensive Guide to Plastic Processing."* This book is for everyone curious about plastic—from engineers and industry professionals to students and entrepreneurs. It dives deep into the world of plastic processing.

Who Will Benefit

> ➤ *Industry Professionals:*

Whether you are a seasoned veteran or just entering the field, this book provides insights that will enhance your proficiency in plastic processing techniques, allowing you to stay at the forefront of industry advancements.

> ➤ *Students and Educators:*

Aspiring engineers and students in plastics and manufacturing programs will find this book to be an invaluable resource. It bridges the gap between theoretical knowledge and practical application, making complex concepts accessible and applicable.

> ➤ *Entrepreneurs and Innovators:*

For those venturing into the realm of plastics entrepreneurship or product development, "Melt to Mold" offers a roadmap, guiding you through the intricacies of material selection, processing methods, and quality control.

Book Perspective

"Melt to Mold" is not just a guide; it's an exploration into the heart of plastic processing. It provides a holistic perspective, covering the fundamentals of raw materials, the nuances of processing methods, the artistry in mold and die design, and the critical aspects of quality control. As we delve into advanced manufacturing technologies and the future landscape of the industry, the book encourages a forward-thinking mindset, embracing sustainability, innovation, and collaboration.

This journey from the melting of raw materials to the meticulous molding of products is a narrative crafted with precision and passion. It's a resource that transforms technical knowledge into practical wisdom, empowering individuals to tackle the complexities of plastic processing with confidence and vision.

Welcome to a comprehensive guide that not only educates but inspires – "Melt to Mold."

Chapter 1

Understanding Plastic Processing

In this chapter, we introduce the world of plastic processing and explain the various types of plastics along with their properties. We will also discuss the different types of processing methods and their applications. This chapter offers a broad overview of the plastic processing industry and serves as a foundation for the rest of the book.

Processing plastic polymers involves converting raw plastic materials into finished products. The specific process used depends on the type of polymer, the desired product properties, and the production volume. Here is a brief overview of the steps involved in plastic polymer processing:

1# **_Material Selection:_** Choose the appropriate plastic polymer for the desired product based on factors such as mechanical properties, chemical resistance, and cost.

2# **_Mechanical Properties:_** Consider the mechanical properties required for the product, such as strength, stiffness, and impact resistance. Different polymers have different properties and can be selected based on the specific requirements.

3# **_Chemical Resistance:_** If the product will be exposed to chemicals or other substances, consider the chemical resistance of the polymer to ensure it will not degrade or break down over time.

4# **_Temperature Resistance:_** If the product will be exposed to high or low temperatures, consider the temperature resistance of the polymer to prevent melting or brittleness.

5# **_Cost:_** Consider the overall cost of the polymer, including raw material and processing costs, to ensure the product is cost-effective.

6# **_Environmental Impact:_** Assess the environmental impact of the polymer, such as its recyclability and biodegradability to ensure the product is sustainable and environmentally friendly.

7# *Appearance:* Address the appearance requirements of the product, such as colour and texture. Choose a polymer that can be easily coloured or textured to achieve the desired appearance.

8# *Processing Method:* Factor in the processing method required for the product, such as injection moulding or extrusion, and choose a polymer that can be easily processed using the chosen method.

Engineering Plastic	Tensile Strength (MPa)	Flexural Strength (MPa)	Impact Strength (J/m)	Heat Deflection Temperature (°C)	Chemical Resistance
ABS	40-60	60-80	100-400	80-100	Good
Polycarbonate (PC)	60-80	80-100	700-900	130-140	Excellent
Polyethylene (PE)	20-30	25-40	20-40	50-60	Good
Polypropylene (PP)	30-40	30-40	20-40	80-100	Excellent
Polyamide (Nylon)	50-90	70-120	50-100	80-100	Good
Polyethylene Terephthalate (PET)	60-80	70-90	20-40	70-80	Excellent
Polyvinyl Chloride (PVC)	45-60	60-80	15-50	70-80	Good
Polyoxymethylene (POM)	60-80	80-100	100-200	80-90	Excellent
Polytetrafluoroethylene (PTFE)	20-30	20-40	5-20	260	Excellent
Polyphenylene Oxide (PPO)	60-80	70-90	60-100	110	Good

Chapter 2

Polymer Preparation

Before processing plastic polymers, it is essential to properly prepare the material to ensure consistent quality and performance. Here are the general steps involved in preparing polymer for processing:

- ➢ **Drying:** Many plastic polymers are hygroscopic, meaning they absorb moisture from the environment. Moisture absorption can lead to defects in the finished product, so it is important to dry the polymer before processing. The drying time and temperature depend on the type of polymer and

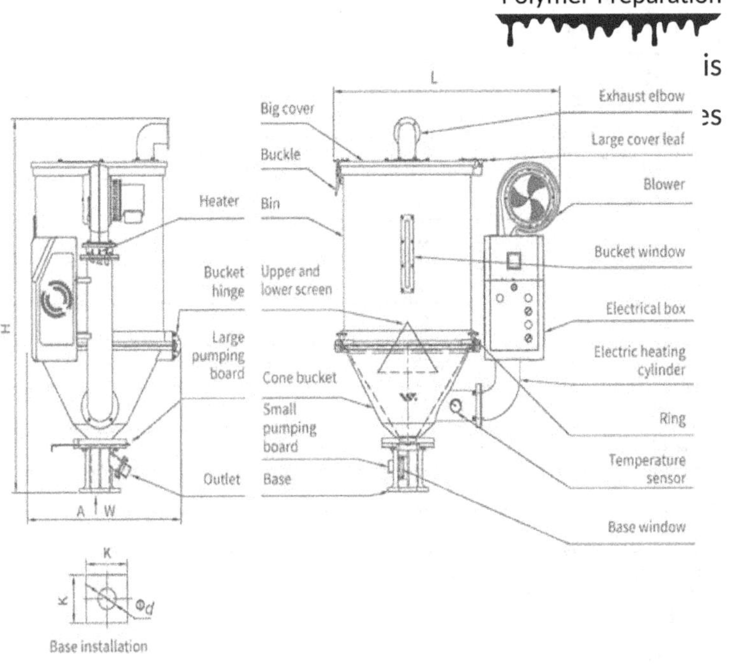

Drying Times

Plastic Material Abbrev.	Drying Temperature(°C)	Drying Time(hrs)
ABS	80~90	2~3
ABS/PC	100~120	2~4
AS	75~85	2~4
ASA	80~90	2.5~3.6
ASA/PC	100~110	3~4
CA	70~80	2~3
CAB	70~80	2~3
EVA	40~50	2~4
GPPS	60~70	2~3

HIPS	60~80	2~4
LCP	150	4
PA6(NY6)	75~100	4~6
PA6(NY6)+GF	75~80	4~6
PA66(NY66)	80~90	3~6
PA10(NY10)	80	4~6
PA11(NY11)	75~80	3~5
PA12(NY12)	75~80	3~5
PBT	120~140	3~4
PBT+GF	120~140	3~4
PC	100~120	2~4
PE	85~90	1
PEEK	140~150	2~4
PEI	150	3~4
PEI+GF	120~150	2~4
PES	130~150	2~4
PET	130~140	3~5
PETG	65~70	4~5
PMMA	70~80	3~5
POM	90~110	2~3
PP	60~80	2~3
PPE(PPO)	90~110	2~3
PPE(PPO)+GF	90~120	2~3
PPS	130~150	3~5
PS	75~80	1~2
PSU	130~150	3~4
PU	80~90	2~3
PVC-Rigid	70~80	1
SAN	70~80	2~4

➤ **Mixing:** If the polymer is a blend of multiple materials, it must be mixed thoroughly to ensure consistent properties throughout the material.

➤ **Pelletizing:** The polymer is typically supplied in the form of pellets or powder. If it is in powder form, it may need to be pelletized for easier handling and feeding into the processing equipment.

➤ **Additives:** Additives such as colorants, stabilizers, and lubricants may be added to the polymer to enhance its properties and performance. These should be added in the correct proportions and mixed thoroughly with the polymer.

➤ **Testing:** Before processing begins, the polymer should be tested to ensure it meets the desired specifications. This may include testing for melt flow rate, moisture content, and other relevant properties.

Checking Moisture Content after Drying

Checking the water content in plastic granules is an essential step in plastic processing to ensure the quality of the final product. Here are a few common methods used to measure water content:

1# *Drying Method:*

a. Weigh a sample of plastic granules before and after drying.

b. Place a known weight of the sample in a drying oven at a specific temperature, typically around 80-105°C.

c. Dry the sample for a specific duration, typically 2-4 hours.

d. Weigh the sample again after drying and calculate the weight loss, which represents the water content.

2# *Karl Fischer Titration:*

a. Karl Fischer titration is a widely used method for measuring water content accurately.

b. Dissolve a small sample of the plastic granules in a suitable solvent.

c. Add a Karl Fischer reagent to the solution, reacting with water to produce a measurable change.

d. Use a titration apparatus to determine the exact amount of reagent consumed, indicating the water content.

3# *Infrared Moisture Analyzer:*

a. Infrared moisture analyzers are specialized instruments designed to measure moisture content in solid materials.

b. Place a small sample of the plastic granules in the moisture analyzer.

c. The instrument uses infrared radiation to heat the sample and measures the moisture content based on the resulting vaporization.

Chapter 3

Plastic Processing Method

There are several processing methods used for plastic polymers, each with its own advantages and disadvantages. The choice of the processing method depends on factors such as the desired product properties, production volume, and cost. Here are some commonly used processing methods for plastic polymers:

→ **Injection Moulding:** This process involves melting plastic pellets and injecting them into a mould under high pressure to produce complex and intricate parts. It is widely used for high-volume production of products such as Consumer Goods, Toys, Electrical & Electronics Components, Construction Fittings, Medical Device, Food Packaging and Automotive Components.

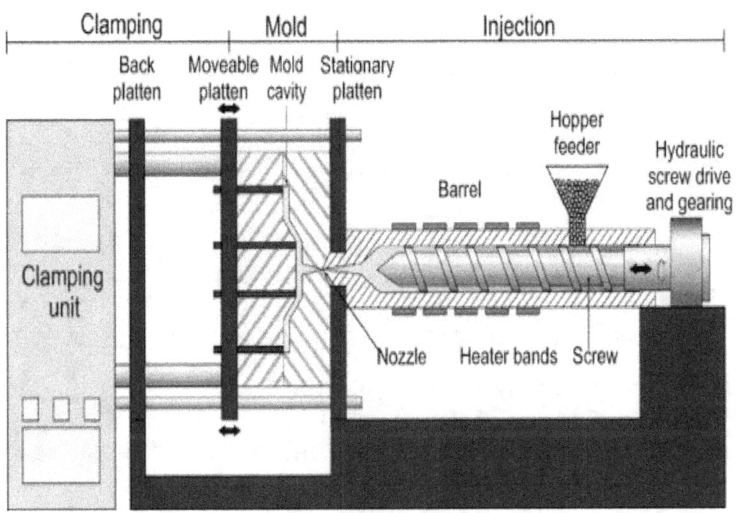

Mainly, there are four types of Clamping Units in an Injection Moulding Machine:

1#   5 Point Toggle Clamping (Clamping unit illustrated in the picture below)

The toggle clamping unit is one of the most common types of clamping mechanisms used in injection molding machines. This mechanism utilizes a series of levers and pivots to multiply the force applied to open and close the mold.

Advantages of a Toggle Clamping Unit:

    a. It can generate a high clamping force with relatively little force input.

    b. It allows for fast movements, thus resulting in shorter cycle times.

    c. It is mechanically simple and,therefore, often more economical.

2# Hydraulic Clamping System (Clamping unit illustrated in the picture below)

In a hydraulic clamping unit, this is achieved using hydraulic cylinders that apply force to the mould.

Advantages of Hydraulic Clamping Units in Injection Moulding Machines:

→ **Force Precision:** Hydraulic systems can produce extremely high clamping forces, and these forces can be precisely controlled.

→ **Durability and Reliability:** Hydraulic clamping units are known for their durability and reliability.

→ **Cost-Effectiveness:** When it comes to the initial investment, hydraulic machines often have a lower price point compared to all-electric or hybrid machines.

➤ ***Peak Force Capability:*** Hydraulic clamps can generate peak forces for short durations without causing any damage to the system. This is particularly useful when processing materials that require high injection pressures.

➤ ***Flexibility:*** Hydraulic machines can be more flexible in terms of process adjustment.

3#   All Electric Clamping Unit:

Electric clamping units use servo motors to actuate the opening and closing of the mold. This contrasts with traditional hydraulic clamping units, which rely on hydraulic fluid and pressure to move the mold.

Here are some key points about electric clamping units:

a. ***Precision:*** Electric clamping allows for highly precise control over the mold position which can improve the molding process's accuracy and repeatability.

b. ***Speed:*** These units can operate more quickly than hydraulic ones, as the response time of electric servo motors is faster.

c. ***Energy Efficiency:*** Electric units consume energy only when they are actively moving the mold.

d. **Clean Operation:** Without hydraulic oil, electric clamping units are cleaner, reducing the risk of contaminating molded parts or the production environment. This is particularly beneficial in industries where cleanliness is paramount, such as in medical device manufacturing.

e. **Maintenance:** Electric units typically require less maintenance than hydraulic units since there are fewer fluid-related issues and no need for oil changes.

4# *Hybrid Clamping Unit:*

Hybrid clamping units incorporate both electric and hydraulic features. These units aim to combine the best of both worlds—electric efficiency and precision with hydraulic power and force.

Key aspects include:

a. **Efficient Use of Hydraulics:** In a hybrid system, hydraulics are often used for the phases of the clamping cycle that require high force, while electric motors handle the phases where precision and speed are more critical.

    b. *Energy Savings:* Although not as energy-efficient as fully electric systems, hybrid clamping units can still offer significant energy savings over traditional hydraulic systems.

    c. *Versatility:* Hybrid units can be more versatile than their all-electric counterparts, as they can generate higher clamping forces when needed. This is important for molding large or complex parts.

    d. *Cost:* Hybrids can sometimes offer a middle-ground solution in terms of cost-effectiveness. They are typically less expensive than all-electric machines but more efficient than hydraulic ones.

Blow Moulding:

This process is used to produce hollow plastic products, such as bottles and containers. The process begins by melting plastic material, shaping it into a tube. This tube is then placed into a mold, and with the help of compressed air, it expands to match the mold's shape. This method offers great flexibility, enabling the production of various container shapes and sizes, making it extremely versatile for manufacturing different types of packaging materials.

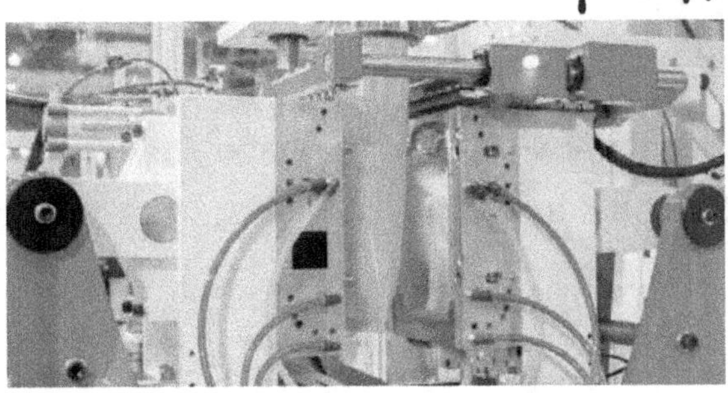

Extrusion:

Extrusion is a manufacturing process that entails pushing molten plastic through a die, resulting in the continuous production of a uniform profile. This versatile method is commonly used to manufacture various products like pipes, tubes, and sheets with consistent dimensions.

Extrusion

- Produces tubes, rods and other shaped continuous form lengths.
- Heated polymer is fed into shaped die by a screw.

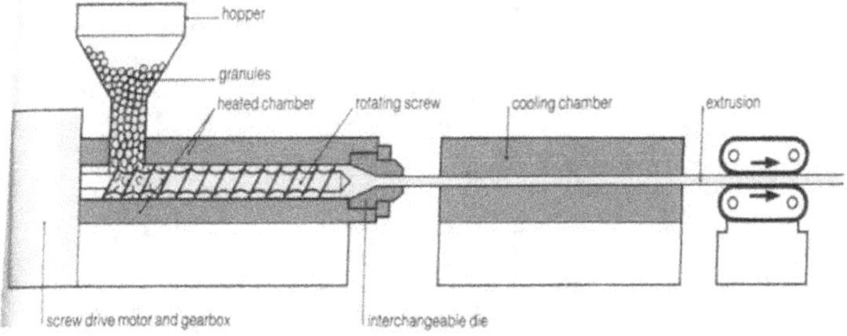

Rotational Moulding:

Rotational moulding, a fascinating process, revolves around the rotation of a mould while heating plastic pellets within. This unique technique gives birth to sizable, hollow components characterized by an even and uniform wall thickness.

Chapter 4

Moulds and Dies

A mould refers to a hollow form or cavity into which molten plastic is injected to give the shape of the required component. The term generally refers to the whole assembly of parts constituting the section of the moulding equipment where the parts are formed. It is also known as a tool or die.

Moulds and dies play a crucial role in plastic processing, shaping raw plastic material into finished products. Here are some of the key roles of moulds and dies in plastic processing:

Cold-runner Mould:

Developed to allow injection of thermoset material either directly into the cavity or through a small sub-runner and gate into the cavity. It may be compared to the hot-runner moulds, with the exception that the manifold section is cooled rather than heated to maintain softened but uncured material. The cavity and core plates are electrically heated to normal moulding temperature and insulated from the cooler manifold section.

Types of Cold Runner Moulds:

There are two major types of cold runner molds: Two-plate and Three-plate.

The main difference between a two-plate mould and a three-plate mould lies in the number of parting planes and their functionality. Here's a breakdown of the distinctions:

1#   *Two-Plate Mould:*

   a. ***Parting Planes:*** A two-plate mould has a single parting plane, which means the mould splits into two halves during the ejection phase.

   b. ***Mould Structure:*** The entire mould is divided into two main plates–the cavity plate (containing the cavity of the final product) and the core plate (housing the core or shape of the product).

   c. ***Gating Locations:*** In a two-plate mould, the runner system must be positioned on the parting plane, restricting the gating locations to the perimeter of the product.

2#   *Three-Plate Mould:*

a. ***Parting Planes:*** A three-plate mould has two parting planes, resulting in three sections when the part is ejected.

b. ***Mould Structure:*** The mould consists of three main plates – the cavity plate, the core plate, and an additional runner plate. The runner plate allows for separation of the runner system from the moulded part.

c. ***Gating Locations:*** The presence of two parting planes in a three-plate mould provides greater flexibility in gating locations. The runner system can be located on one parting plane, while the moulded part is on the other.

Application Differences:

Two-Plate Mould: Simple and commonly used for straightforward injection molding processes. Suited for products with uncomplicated designs and gating requirements.

Three-Plate Mould: Employed in more complex injection molding processes where additional features, gating options, or specific gating positions are necessary. Offers enhanced flexibility for intricate part geometries.

Hot-runner Mould:

A hot-runner mould is an injectionmould in which the runners are kept hot and insulated from the chilled cavities. Plastic freezes-offs occur at gate of cavity; runners are in a separate plate, so they are not, as is usually the case, ejected with the piece. Hot runner moulds are two-plate moulds with a heated runner system inside one half of the mould.

A hot runner system consists of two main components: the manifold and the drops. The manifold comprises channels that transport the plastic along a single plane, parallel to the parting line, reaching a point above the cavity. The drops, positioned perpendicular to the manifold, then convey the plastic from the manifold to the part.

Types of Hot Runner Moulds:

There are many variations of hot runner systems. Typically, hot runner systems are categorized based on the method used to heat the plastic.There are externally and internally heated drops and manifolds.

↠ *Externally Heated Hot Runners/Drops*

Externally heated hot runner channels have the lowest pressure drop of any runner systems.This is due to the absence of a heater obstructing the flow, and all the plastic remains molten. These channels are particularly advantageous for color changes as none of the plastic in the runner system freezes. Moreover, externally heated systems are suitable for thermally sensitive materials, as there are no places for material to hang up and degrade.

⇥ *Internally Heated Hot Runners/Drops*

Internally heated runner systems demand higher moulding pressures, making colour changes more challenging. Numerous locations exist where material can hang up and degrade, rendering them unsuitable for use with thermally sensitive materials.However, internally heated drops offer better gate tip control. Additionally, thesesystems effectively isolate runner heat from the mould due to the formation of an insulating frozen layer against the steel wall on the inside of the flow channels.

Advantages of Hot Runner System Over a Cold Runner System:

- ⇥ *Elimination of Runner Scrap:* Hot runners completely eliminate runner scrap. There are no runners to sort from the parts, and no runners to throw away or regrind and remix into the original material.

- ⇥ *Popularity in High-Production Parts:* Hot runners are popular in high-production parts, particularly those with many cavities.

Additional benefits include:

- ► No runners to disconnect from the molded parts

- ► No runners to remove or regrind, eliminating the need for process/robotics for removal

- ► Reduced Possibility of Contamination

- ► Lower Injection Pressures

- ► Lower Clamping Pressure

- ► Consistent Heat at Processing Temperature within the Cavity

- ► Shorter Cooling Time (as there is no need for thicker, longer-cycle runners)

- ► Reduced Shot Size by Runner Weight

- ► Cleaner Moulding Process (no regrinding necessary)

- ► Elimination of Nozzle Freeze and Sprue Sticking Issues

Disadvantages of Hot Runner System Compared to Cold Runner System:

A hot-runner mold is significantly more expensive than a cold runner. It requires costly maintenance and demands a higher skill level for operation. Color changes with hot

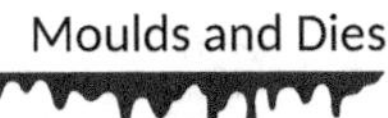

runner molds can be challenging, as it is virtually impossible to remove all the plastic from an internal runner system.

Types of Runners & Gate

→ *Sprue Bushing*

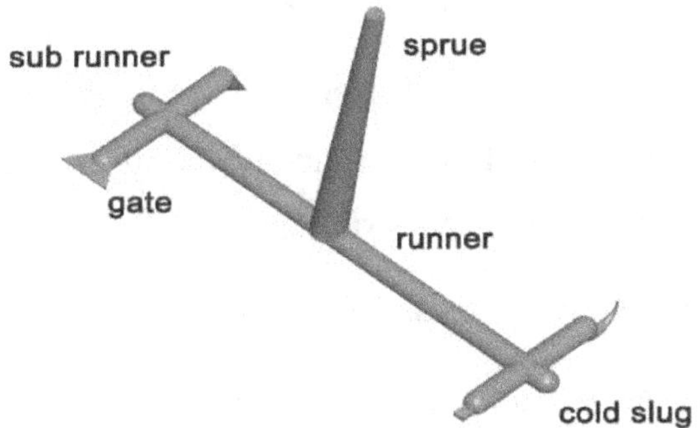

Type of Runners

1#   *Cold Runners:*

a. In cold runner systems, the plastic material is injected into the mold, and excess material solidifies in the channels (runners).

b. After the molding process is complete, the solidified plastic in the runners is usually scrapped or recycled.

c. Cold runners are simple and cost-effective but can generate more waste.

2#   Hot Runners:

a. Hot runner systems use heated channels (runners) to maintain the molten state of the plastic material.

b. This eliminates the need for solidified runners, reducing material waste.

c. Hot runners are more complex and expensive but offer better efficiency and can be more environmentally friendly.

3#   Submarine or Sprue-less Runners:

a. These runners are a variation of hot runners where the sprue which is the main channel feeding the mold, is eliminated.

b. The plastic material is directly injected into the mold cavities through small gates.

c. This reduces waste and simplifies the molding process.

Types of Gates

1#   Sprue Gate:

a. Located at the parting line between the mold halves.

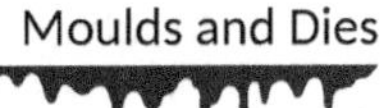

b. Directs molten plastic from the runner system into the mold cavity.

c. Typically used for larger parts.

2# *Runner Gate:*

a. Connects the sprue to the individual mold cavities.

b. Distributes the molten plastic to multiple locations.

c. Comes in various shapes, including edge gates and tab gates.

3# *Edge Gate:*

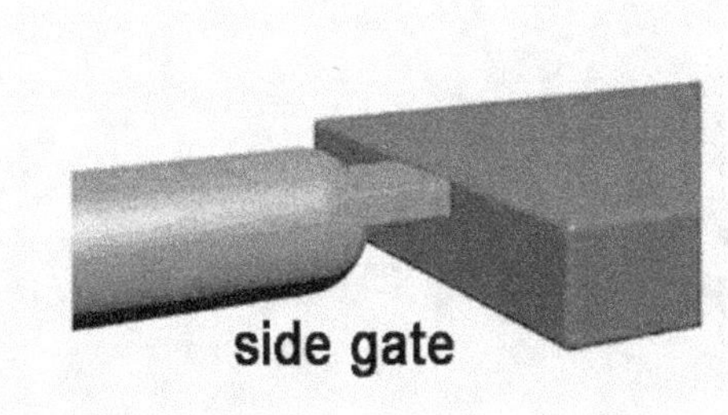

a. A type of runner gate that is located at the edge of the part.

b. It leaves a small scar or mark but is often used for easier removal of the part from the mold.

4#   Tab Gate:

a. Similar to an edge gate but with a small tab of plastic left at the gate location.

b. tab can be easily trimmed during post-processing

5#   Submarine Gate (Banana Gate):

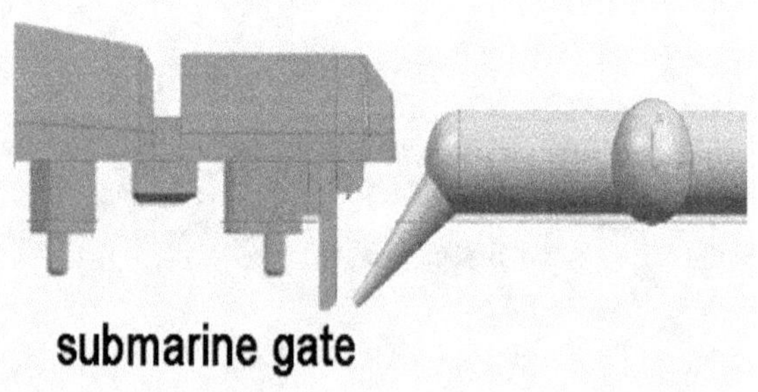

a. A gate placed beneath the part, reducing visible marks on the finished product.

b. Commonly used in cosmetic parts.

6# *Pinpoint Gate:*

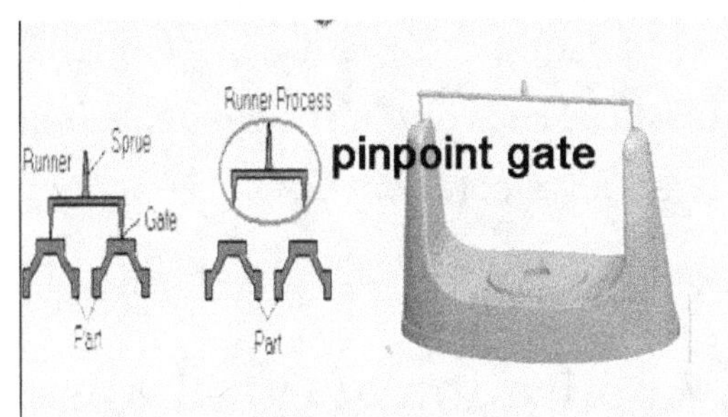

a. A small, pinpoint-sized gate used for precision and to minimize the size of the gate scar.

b. Often used in cosmetic parts where appearance is critical.

7# *Fan Gate:*

a. Distributes plastic in a fan-like pattern.

b. Helps to reduce stress and improve part appearance.

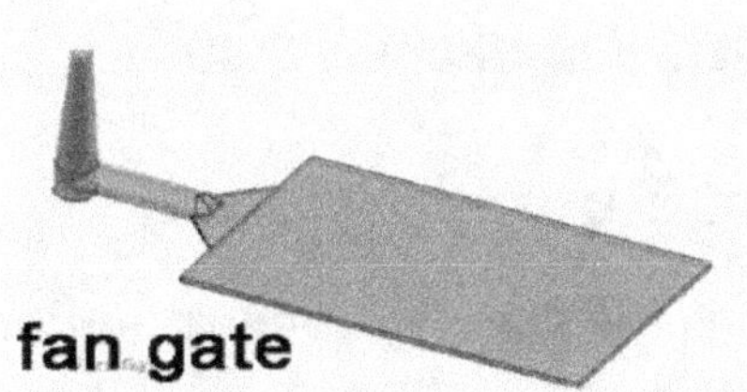

8#   Hot Runner:

a. Not a gate per se, but a system where molten plastic is kept hot in the runner, eliminating the need for a cold runner.

b. Reduces material waste and cycle time

Types & Application of Hot Runners

When applying the hot runner technology, the proper selection of gate type is of critical importance because the gate type directly determines the selection of hot runner components, as well as the manufacturing and application of molds.

Therefore, the hot runner system can be classified into three types based on the gate type, i.e.,

→ Hot Tip Hot Runner System,

→ Sprue Gating Hot Runner System and

→ Valve Gating Hot Runner System.

Hot Tip Hot Runner System:

The hot tip is the standard, general-purpose version of the hot runner system that we have discussed thus far. It is more economical than the valve gate system and is the most commonly used hot runner system. The hot tip is ideal for mass production of simple parts and products.

Sprue Gating Hot Runner System:

In the realm of hot runner systems, the sprue gating hot runner system holds a distinctive place. Unlike the traditional cold runner approach, the sprue gating system involves injecting plastic directly into the mold through a single sprue, eliminating the need for a separate runner system. This method is characterized by its efficiency in reducing material waste, streamlining the molding process, and providing greater flexibility in design.

Valve Gate Hot Runner System:

A valve gate is a type of injection point that incorporates a mechanical valve automatically closing when the machine injects plastic into the mold. This ensures a seamless closure, leaving the product's surface free from any visible nubs or abrasions. A valve gate system is ideal for products that need to look great; highly aesthetic projects noticed by customers. This system is even more efficient than the general-purpose hot runner and, as such, is more expensive.

The Future of Injection Molding:

Although cold runner systems will continue to have their place, it's evident that hot runners represent both current and future technology. The decreased cycle time and elimination of runner waste firmly establish hot runners as essential in contemporary injection molding. Recognizing this, it becomes crucial to discern when to opt for either system. A deeper understanding of hot runner systems and their capabilities empowers better-informed decisions for the years ahead.

Chapter 5

Process Optimization

Key process parameters and their impact on product quality

Key process parameters in plastic processing can significantly impact the quality of the final plastic product. Here are some of the important parameters and their impact:

- → **Temperature:** Temperature control is critical in plastic processing. It affects the melting and flow characteristics of the plastic material. Incorrect temperatures can lead to incomplete melting, improper flow, or degradation of the material, resulting in poor product quality, such as surface defects or dimensional inaccuracies

→ **Pressure:** Pressure plays a crucial role in ensuring proper material flow and filling of the Mold or die. Insufficient pressure can result in incomplete filling, voids, or weak weld lines. Excessive pressure can cause mold damage, flash, or part distortion. Optimal pressure control is essential for achieving the desired product quality.

→ **Injection Speed:** The speed at which the molten plastic is injected into the mold affects the filling pattern, material distribution, and cooling. Improper injection speed can lead to flow marks, sink marks, or short shots, impacting the product's appearance and structural integrity.

→ **Cooling Time and Rate:** Cooling time and rate determine the solidification and cooling of the plastic material within the mold. Proper cooling is crucial for achieving dimensional stability and minimizing internal stresses. Insufficient cooling time or improper cooling rate can result in warpage, sink marks, or part shrinkage.

→ **Cycle Time:** Cycle time refers to the time required for a complete molding cycle, including filling, cooling, and part ejection. Efficient cycle time management is essential for optimizing productivity.

However, excessively short cycle times can affect part quality due to insufficient cooling or premature demolding.

→ **Material Moisture Content:** Moisture content in plastic materials can affect the flow behavior, material properties, and part quality. Excessive moisture can lead to surface defects, voids, or dimensional variations. Proper material drying and moisture control are crucial for consistent product quality.

→ **Screw Speed and Back Pressure (for Refilling):** In extrusion processes, screw speed and back pressure impact the melting, mixing, and extrusion of the plastic material. Improper screw speed or excessive back pressure can lead to material degradation, poor mixing, or unstable extrusion, resulting in product defects.

→ **Holding Pressure and Time (for Injection Moulding):** Holding pressure and time refer to the pressure applied to the material during the solidification phase. Proper holding pressure and time are critical for maintaining part dimensions, minimizing sink marks, and ensuring complete filling of complex geometries.

→ ***Mold and Die Design:*** The design of the mold or die, including gate location, venting, cooling channels, and ejection system, can significantly impact product quality. A well-designed mold or die ensures proper material flow, minimizes warpage, and facilitates easy part release.

Process monitoring and control

Process monitoring and control play a crucial role in ensuring the quality, efficiency, and consistency of plastic processing operations. Here are some key aspects of process monitoring and control in plastics:

→ ***Process Parameters:*** Monitoring and controlling process parameters, such as temperature, pressure, cooling rate, melt flow rate, and cycle time, are essential for achieving desired product properties. This can be accomplished through sensors and automated control systems.

→ ***Real-time Monitoring:*** Continuous monitoring of process parameters helps identify any deviations or variations during production. It allows operators to take corrective actions promptly and prevent defects or quality issues.

→ ***Statistical Process Control (SPC):*** SPC involves collecting and analysing data from the production process to understand process variations and trends. Statistical techniques, such as control charts, are used to monitor and control the process, ensuring it stays within acceptable limits.

→ ***Quality Assurance:*** Process monitoring and control help ensure product quality by detecting and addressing any variations that may lead to defects or non-conformities. This includes monitoring critical dimensions, material consistency, and visual inspection during the production process.

→ ***Closed-Loop Control Systems:*** Closed-loop control systems automatically adjust process parameters based on real-time feedback from sensors and measurements. This enables precise control and optimization of the process, reducing waste, and improving efficiency.

→ ***Process Validation:*** Regular validation of the process ensures that it remains within specified tolerances and meets quality standards. This involves conducting tests, measurements, and inspections to verify the process performance and consistency.

> → ***Human-Machine Interface (HMI):*** Advanced plastic processing machines are equipped with user-friendly HMIs that allow operators to monitor and control the process parameters, set alarms for deviations, and adjust parameters as needed.

> → ***Automation and Robotics:*** The integration of automation and robotics in plastic processing enables more precise and consistent control of process parameters. It reduces human error and allows for faster and more efficient production.

> → ***Data Analysis and Optimization:*** Process monitoring data can be analyzed to identify trends, optimize process parameters, and improve overall production efficiency. Advanced analytics and machine learning techniques can uncover insights and patterns for continuous process improvement.

Trouble Shooting

> → ***Moulding defects***

Injection moulding is a complex technology that may encounterproduction problems. They can be caused either by defects in the moulds, or more often, by the moulding process itself.[3]: 47-85

Moulding defects	Descriptions	Causes
Blister	A raised or layered zone on the surface of the part	This issue occurs when the tool or material is too hot, often caused by a lack of cooling around the tool or a faulty heater.
Burn marks	Black or brown burnt areas on the part located at furthest points from the gate or where air is trapped.	This problem arises when the tool lacks venting, or the injection speed is too high.
Colour streaks	Localised change of colour on the part	This can happen when the Masterbatch isn't mixing properly, or the material has run out and 'is starting to come through as natural only. Previous coloured material "dragging" in the nozzle or check valve.
Contamination	Different colored matter seen in product, weakening the product	This issue is caused by the poor material introduced through a bad recycling or regrind policy; may include floor sweepings, dust, and debris.
Delamination	Thin mica-like layers formed in the part wall	Delamination occurs due to contamination of the material, e.g., PP mixed with ABSThis is particularly very dangerous if the part is being used for a safety-critical application, as the material has very little strength when delaminated since the materials cannot bond.

Flash	Excess material in thin layer exceeding normal part geometry	Flash can result from the mould being over packed, damageto the parting line on the tool, too much injection speed/ material injection, or insufficient clamping force. It can also be caused by dirt and contaminants around tooling surfaces.
Embedded contaminates	Foreign particles (burnt material or other) embedded in the part	This issue may arise from particles on the tool surface, contaminated material, foreign debris in the barrel, or excessive shear heat burning the material prior to injection.
Flow marks	Directionally "off tone" wavy lines or patterns	This occurs when injection speeds too slow; the plastic has cooled down too much during injection.Set injection speeds to the maximum suitable rate for the chosen process and material.
Gate Blush	Circular pattern around the gate, normally only an issue on hot runner molds	This arises when the injection speed is too fast, the gate/ sprue/runner size is too small, or the melt/mold temp is too low.
Jetting	Jetting refers to a snake-like stream that occurs when molten polymer is forcefully pushed through restricted areas at high velocity.	This can result from poor tool design, gate position or runner or when the injection speed is set too high. Poor design of gates, which causes too little die swell, can also lead to jetting.

Knit lines	Thin lines on the reverse side of core pins or within parts, resembling simple linear features.	These are caused by the melt-front flowing around an object standing proud in a plastic part, as well as at the end of fill where the melt-front comes together again. This flaw can be minimised or eliminated with a mould-flow study when the mould is in design phase. After the mold is created and the gate is set, the only way to reduce this imperfection is by adjusting both the melt and mold temperature.
Polymer degradation	Polymer breakdown from hydrolysis, oxidation, etc.	This can occur due to excess water in the granules, excessive temperatures in the barrel, excessive screw speeds causing high shear heat, or allowing the material to sit in the barrel for too long. Additionally, too much regrind being usedcan contribute to polymer degradation.
Sink marks	`Localised depression (In thicker zones)	Holding time/pressure too low, cooling time too short, or, with sprueless hot runners, this can also be caused by the gate temperature being set too high. Sink marks may also occur due to excessive material or walls too thick.
Short shot	Partial part	This problem is attributed to a lack of material, injection speed or pressure too low, the mould being too cold, or a lack of gas vents.

Splay marks	Typically manifests as silver streaks following the flow pattern, but the appearance may vary based on the material type and color; in some cases, it might resemble small bubbles resulting from trapped moisture.	This issue is typically associated with moisture in the material, usually when hygroscopic resins are dried improperly. Trapping of gas in "rib" areas due to excessive injection velocity in these areas,material being too hot, or being sheared too much can contribute to splay marks.
Stringiness	String-like remnants from the previous shot transferring into the new shot.	This occurs when the nozzle temperature is too high,the gate hasn't frozen off, there is no decompression of the screw, no sprue break, or there is poor placement of the heater bands inside the tool.
Voids	Empty space within the part (commonly referred to as an air pocket)	The lack of pack pressure (pack pressure is used to pack out the part during the holding time) contributes to this issue. Filling too fast doesn't cause this condition; rather, a void is a sink that didn't have a place to happen. As the part shrinks, the resin separates from itself due to insufficient resin in the cavity. Voids can occur at any area of the part, not limited by thickness but influenced by resin flow and thermal conductivity.Thicker areas like ribs or bosses are more prone to voids. Additional root causes for voids include unmelted material in the melt pool.

Weld line	A discoloured line where two flow fronts meet.	This problem may result from mould or material temperatures being set too low,causing the material to be cold when they meet and preventing proper bonding. It can also be influenced by the transition time between injection and transfer (to packing and holding) being too early.
Warping	Distorted part	Warping can occur due to insufficient cooling time, material being too hot, lack of cooling around the tool, or incorrect water temperatures (the parts bow inwards towards the hot side of the tool). Uneven shrinking between different areas of the part can also contribute to warping.
Cracks	Improper fusion of two fluid flows, a state before weld line.	Cracks or threadline gaps between parts can result fromimproper gate location in complex design parts, including an excess of holes (multipoint gates to be provided).Process optimization and proper air venting are essential for minimizing this issue.

Chapter 6

Quality Control

Importance of quality control in plastic processing:

→ **Quality Control:** Throughout the process, quality control measures must be implemented to ensure the final product meets the desired specifications.

- ▶ Visual Control

- ▶ Mechanical Control

- ▶ Weight Control

- ▶ Dimensional Stability

- ▶ Stress Control

- ▶ Viscosity Control

Standards & Regulations:

Standards and regulations play a critical role in ensuring the quality and safety of plastic parts. Here are some of the key standards and regulations relevant to quality control in the production of plastic parts:

- → **ISO 9001:** This is an international standard for quality management systems. It provides a framework for organizations to establish and maintain effective quality management practices, including the production of plastic parts.

- → **ISO/TS 16949:** This standard specifically focuses on quality management in the automotive industry. It outlines requirements for organizations involved in the design, development, production, and service of automotive-related products, including plastic parts.

- → **ASTM International Standards:** ASTM International develops and publishes voluntary consensus standards for various industries, including plastics. These standards cover a wide range of topics related to plastics, such as material properties, testing methods, and product specifications.

→ ***RoHS (Restriction of Hazardous Substances):*** The RoHS directive restricts the use of certain hazardous substances in electrical and electronic equipment, including plastic components. It aims to reduce the environmental impact and potential health risks associated with these substances.

→ ***REACH (Registration, Evaluation, Authorization, and Restriction of Chemicals):*** REACH is a regulation of the European Union that addresses the production and use of chemicals, including those used in plastic manufacturing. It aims to ensure the safe handling and use of chemicals and promotes the substitution of hazardous substances with safer alternatives.

→ ***FDA (Food and Drug Administration) Regulations:*** In industries such as food packaging and medical devices, plastic parts must comply with FDA regulations to ensure they are safe for their intended use. These regulations specify requirements for materials, manufacturing processes, and product performance.

→ ***UL (Underwriters Laboratories) Standards:*** UL develops safety standards and conducts testing and certification for various products, including plastic parts used in electrical and electronic applications.

Compliance with UL standards assures the safety and reliability of these products.

It's important for manufacturers to be aware of and adhere to relevant standards and regulations applicable to their specific industry and product requirements. Compliance with these standards helps ensure the quality, performance, and safety of plastic parts and promotes customer confidence.

Chapter 7

Post-processing and Finishing

With injection moulding, there are six common types of post-processing activities.

1#   Gate Trimming

Flash mars the finish of moulded parts and can interfere with sealing, and assembly. Typically, this surface defect occurs when excess plastic is forced from a mould cavity at the parting line or ejector pin locations. Effective tooling for quality control minimizes the creation of flash, although secondary gate trimming may still be necessary.

Gates are openings that allow the molten plastic to enter the mould cavity. While the majority of the plastic solidifies within the cavity to shape the part, there is some material that solidifies at the gates and protrudes. Gate trimming, or degating, removes these protrusions either inside the injection moulding machine or after the part has been ejected.

2#   Painting

Painting is a versatile post-processing method that enhances the visual appeal and functionality of injection-molded parts. This technique allows for the application of a wide range of colors, finishes, and even intricate designs onto the surface of molded components. Painting serves not only aesthetic purposes but also functional ones, such as providing additional protection against environmental factors or adding specific properties like conductivity or insulation.

There are various painting methods available for injection-molded parts, each offering unique advantages:

- *Spray Painting:* This is the simplest process and can use self-curing paints that air-dry. You can find paints that come in two parts and cure through exposure to ultraviolet (UV) light.

- *Powder Coating:* This method applies a powdered plastic and requires UV curing to ensure surface adhesion and to help avoid chipping and flaking.

➢ ***Silk Screening:*** This technique is used when parts need two different colors. To keep certain areas unpainted, a screen is employed to cover or conceal them when applying each color.

3#   *Laser Marking*

Laser marking is a precise and efficient method used to engrave or mark injection-molded parts with information such as serial numbers, logos, or barcodes. The process involves using a laser beam to remove or modify the material's surface, leaving a permanent and high-contrast mark. Laser marking is especially valuable for applications where durability and readability of the marking are essential. This method is often used in industries such as electronics, automotive, and medical devices.

4#   *Pad Printing*

Pad printing is a versatile technique used for transferring 2D images onto 3D surfaces. A silicone pad is used to transfer ink from an engraved metal plate to the surface of the molded part. This method is suitable for intricate designs and irregular shapes, making it widely used in industries like consumer electronics, automotive, and medical devices. Pad printing allows for the application of fine details and multiple colors, providing a high level of customization.

5# *Heat Staking*

Heat staking is a process used to join plastic parts through localized heating and forming. Typically, a heated metal or plastic stake is pressed against the part, creating a bond at specific points. This method is commonly employed for assembling parts that have features such as clips, tabs, or bosses. Heat staking is widely used in industries like automotive, electronics, and consumer goods for assembling components without the need for additional fasteners.

6# *Ultrasonic Welding*

Ultrasonic welding is a fast and efficient method of joining thermoplastic components. It involves using high-frequency ultrasonic vibrations to generate heat at the joint interface, melting the plastic and creating a strong bond as it cools. This process is particularly useful for welding intricate or small parts and is commonly used in the automotive, medical, and electronics industries. Ultrasonic welding offers advantages such as speed, precision, and the ability to join dissimilar materials.

Within each process, there may be variations. For example, there is more than one way to paint injection-moulded parts. By understanding all your options, you can choose the right post-processing for your next project.

Recycling

Sprues & Faulty rejected moulding parts produced from different raw materials can be reground with minimal reduction in properties. Care should be taken to ensure that reground material is not degraded & is clean & free from impurities.

Special attention is required that ensure that reground material isn't used for impact-critical applications.Blends of reground and new material are possible in the ratio of up to 20/80. It is important that reground materials are properly dried prior to moulding.

Chapter 8

Case Studies

Case studies of Successful Plastic Processing Operations

Case Study 1:

Enhancing Efficiency in Automotive Component Manufacturing at VBros Pvt. Ltd. with Hinds Plastic Machines Pvt. Ltd.

Client: VBros Pvt. Ltd.

→ *Background*

VBros Pvt. Ltd., a leading automotive component manufacturing company, was facing challenges in meeting the increasing demand for their products while simultaneously striving to reduce operational costs, particularly in the context of labor-intensive processes. In their pursuit of innovative solutions, they approached Hinds Plastic Machines Pvt. Ltd., a renowned provider of injection molding technology.

⇥ *Client's Challenge*

VBros Pvt. Ltd. aimed to boost production efficiency, cut down on labor costs, and enhance overall operational effectiveness. They sought a solution that could streamline their manufacturing processes, with a focus on optimizing part placement and retrieval during injection molding.

⇥ Hinds Plastic Machines Pvt. Ltd.'s Proposal

Understanding the specific needs of VBros', Hinds Plastic Machines proposed the integration of robotic automation into their injection molding processes. The proposed solution involved the installation of a state-of-the-art robotic system on the HINDS injection molding machine Euro TS 200-ton model. This robotic system was designed to efficiently handle tasks related topart placement and retrieval, ultimately optimizing the production line and reducing the dependency on manual labor.

Implementation Process

⇥ ***Assessment and Customization:*** Hinds Plastic Machines conducted a thorough assessment of VBros' existing production setup, identifying key

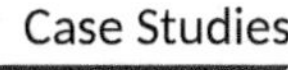

areas for improvement. The robotic system was then customized to seamlessly integrate with the Euro TS 200-ton injection molding machine.

→ **_Robotics Integration:_** The Hinds team, in collaboration with VBros' engineering team, meticulously integrated the robotic system into the injection molding process. The robot was programmed for precise part placement and pick-up, ensuring accuracy and efficiency in the manufacturing cycle.

→ **_Testing and Optimization:_** Rigorous testing was conducted to ensure the seamless operation of the robotic system with the injection molding machine. Fine-tuning and optimization were carried out to maximize efficiency and minimize cycle times.

→ **_Employee Training:_** VBros' staff received comprehensive training on operating and maintaining the newly integrated robotic system. This training aimed to empower the workforce to adapt to the technological advancements and oversee the automated processes effectively.

Results and Benefits

- → ***Increased Production Capacity:*** The integration of the robotic system significantly enhanced the overall production capacity of VBros. The automated processes streamlined production, allowing for higher output without compromising on quality.

- → ***Labor Cost Reduction:*** By automating part placement and retrieval, VBros experienced a notable reduction in labor costs. The need for manual intervention in these repetitive tasks was minimized, leading to cost savings for the company.

- → ***Improved Precision and Quality:*** The robotic system ensured consistent and precise part placement, contributing to a reduction in defects and an overall improvement in product quality. This had a positive impact on customer satisfaction and reduced rework costs.

- → ***Enhanced Operational Efficiency:*** The combination of the HINDS injection molding machine and the integrated robotic system optimized the entire manufacturing process. Cycle times were reduced, downtime was minimized, and operational efficiency was significantly enhanced.

Conclusion

The collaboration between VBros Pvt. Ltd. and Hinds Plastic Machines Pvt. Ltd. shows how using robots in manufacturing can be successful. Adding robotic technology not only solved VBros' problems right away but also set them up for long-term success by using the latest methods in injection molding. This example proves how new technology can make operations smoother, boost efficiency, and lead to overall business success.

Case Study2:

Enhancing Efficiency in Food Packaging with In-Mould Labelling Automation

Client: M/s. Royal Packaging (Bawana, Delhi)

Client's Challenge

M/s. Royal Packaging, a leading food packaging company based in Bawana, Delhi, approached Hinds Plastic Machines Pvt. Ltd. with a key challenge - to increase production efficiency and simultaneously reduce manpower costs. With a focus on delivering high-quality food packaging solutions, the client was looking for an innovative approach to streamline their processes.

Hinds Plastic Machines Pvt. Ltd.'s Solution

Hinds Plastic Machines Pvt. Ltd., a renowned player in the plastic processing machinery sector, proposed a comprehensive solution to address the client's challenges. The solution involved the integration of In-Mould Labelling (IML) technology with a robotic system on their state-of-the-art injection moulding machine, the Euro TS 160-ton machine.

Key Components of the Solution

Euro TS 160 Ton Injection Moulding Machine:

- ➤ Hinds Plastic Machines provided M/s. Royal Packaging with the Euro TS 160-ton injection moulding machine, renowned for its precision, reliability, and efficiency.

- ➤ The Euro TS series comes with advanced features that guarantee optimal performance in high-speed and high-precision injection moulding.

- ➤ In-Mould Labelling Technology:

- ➤ The inclusion of In-Mould Labelling (IML) allows for the integration of labels directly into the packaging during the moulding process.

→ IML not only enhances the aesthetics of the packaging but also eliminates the need for secondary labelling processes, saving time and resources.

Robotic System for Label Placement:

→ Hinds Plastic Machines integrated a sophisticated robotic system with the Euro TS 160-ton machine for precise and efficient label placement during the injection moulding process.

→ The robotic system ensures speed, accuracy, and consistency in the placement of labels on the packaging.

Benefits Realized by M/s. Royal Packaging:

Increased Production Efficiency:

→ The integration of IML with the Euro TS 160-ton machine significantly increased the overall production efficiency for M/s. Royal Packaging.

→ Simultaneous labelling and moulding reduced cycle times, resulting in higher output without compromising on quality.

Manpower Reduction:

→ Automation through the robotic system led to a substantial reduction in manual labour requirements.

→ M/s. Royal Packaging experienced cost savings associated with a reduced workforce, as well as a decline in human error.

Enhanced Product Aesthetics:

→ In-Mould Labelling technology improved the visual appeal of the packaging by ensuring seamless and high-quality label integration.

→ The Euro TS 160-ton machine's precision played a vital role in maintaining product consistency.

Operational Flexibility:

→ The integrated system provided M/s. Royal Packaging with operational flexibility, allowing quick changeovers between different label designs and packaging requirements.

Conclusion

Hinds Plastic Machines Pvt. Ltd.'s innovative solution empowered M/s. Royal Packaging to not only meet their production goals but also to achieve a competitive edge in the food packaging industry. The successful implementation of In-Mould Labelling with a robotic system on the Euro TS 160-ton machine showcased the potential of advanced plastic processing technologies in transforming traditional manufacturing processes into streamlined, efficient, and cost-effective operations.

Case Study 3:

Revolutionizing ETT Cuff Manufacturing in India with the Introduction of a Hybrid Blow Moulding Machine

Client: M/s. Sterimed Surgical India Pvt. Ltd. (Bahadhurgarh)

Client Background

Sterimed Surgical India Pvt. Ltd., a leading medical equipment manufacturer in India, specializes in producing high-quality surgical and medical products. With a commitment to innovation and a focus on meeting global standards, Sterimed identified an opportunity to enhance their endotracheal tube (ETT) cuff manufacturing process.

Challenge

The client faced challenges in sourcing advanced blow moulding machines for ETT cuff production, relying heavily on imports from China. This not only posed logistical challenges but also raised concerns regarding dependency on a single source.

Objectives

- ➢ Innovate and design an advanced Hybrid Blow Moulding Machine specifically designed for the manufacturing of ETT cuffs.

- ➢ Establish domestic manufacturing of the machine to reduce dependency on imports.

- ➢ Improve production efficiency, quality, and flexibility for enhanced manufacturing capabilities.

Solution

Conceptualization and Design:

- ➢ We developed the concept of Hybrid Blow Moulding Machine that combines the benefits of both extrusion blow moulding and Servo blow moulding technologies.

➤ Focused on creating a versatile machine capable of producing high-quality ETT cuffs with precision and efficiency.

Design & Development:

➤ Understand the concept of the Blow moulding machine & design the Hybrid Blow Moulding Machine, with a double station driven by Servo motors, integrating cutting-edge technology for precise control over the Extrusion & Blowing process.

➤ Conducted rigorous testing to ensure the machine's compatibility with PVC materials, including medical-grade plastics required for ETT cuff production.

➤ We collaborated closely with Sterimed throughout the development process to understand their specific requirements and incorporate necessary features into the machine.

➤ Additionally, we provided training to Sterimed's engineers for operating and maintaining the Hybrid Blow Moulding Machine.

Results

→ ***Domestic Manufacturing Capability:*** Sterimed gained the ability to manufacture Hybrid Blow Moulding Machines domestically, eliminating the need to depend solely on imports.

→ ***Enhanced Production Efficiency:*** The Hybrid Blow Moulding Machine proved to be highly efficient, allowing Sterimed to increase production capacity while maintaining high-quality standards.

→ ***Reduced Costs:*** By manufacturing the machine in India, Sterimed experienced cost savings in terms of logistics and import duties, contributing to overall profitability.

→ ***Market Leadership:*** Sterimed positioned itself as a market leader by introducing innovative, locally manufactured machinery, showcasing a commitment to self-sufficiency and technological advancement.

Conclusion

The successful collaboration between the engineering team and Sterimed Surgical India Pvt. Ltd. resulted in the development of a groundbreaking Hybrid Blow Moulding Machine. This not only addressed the client's immediate challenges but also positioned Sterimed as a pioneer in medical equipment manufacturing in India. The establishment of a domestic manufacturing unit not only contributed to the client's operational efficiency but also strengthened the resilience of the Indian medical equipment industry.

Chapter 9

Future of Plastic Processing

Emerging trends and technologies in the plastics processing industry are constantly evolving, driven by the need for increased efficiency, sustainability, and product innovation. Here are some of the notable trends and technologies shaping the future of plastics processing:

1#   Industry 4.0 and Automation:

a. Integration of automation, robotics, and data-driven systems for enhanced productivity and efficiency.

b. Smart manufacturing techniques, such as real-time monitoring, predictive maintenance, and remote operation.

2#   *Additive Manufacturing (3D Printing):*

    a. Advancements in 3D printing technology for rapid prototyping and production of complex plastic parts.

    b. Development of new materials and printing processes to enhance strength, durability, and functional properties.

3#   *Sustainable Materials and Processes:*

    a. Growing emphasis on environmentally friendly materials, such as bioplastics and biodegradable polymers.

    b. Adoption of recycling technologies and closed-loop systems to minimize waste and resource consumption.

4#   *Advanced Composite Materials:*

    a. Incorporation of reinforcing fibers, nanoparticles, and fillers to enhance the mechanical, thermal, and electrical properties of plastics.

    b. Development of lightweight and high-strength composites for automotive, aerospace, and construction applications.

5# *Advanced Molding and Processing Techniques:*

a. Use of micro-injection molding for the production of miniature and precision parts.

b. Multi-component molding, insert molding, and overmolding techniques for complex part designs and functional integration.

6# Digitalization and Simulation:

a. Virtual prototyping and simulation tools to optimize designs, predict material behavior, and reduce time-to-market.

b. Digital twin technology for real-time monitoring, optimization, and predictive maintenance of production processes.

7# Energy Efficiency and Process Optimization:

a. Implementation of energy-efficient machinery, heat recovery systems, and process optimization techniques to reduce energy consumption and costs.

b. Adoption of advanced process control systems to achieve tighter process tolerances and improve product quality.

8#   *Bio-inspired Design and Manufacturing:*

a. Application of biomimicry principles to develop innovative designs and manufacturing processes inspired by nature.

b. Exploration of natural materials and structures to enhance material properties, sustainability, and functional performance.

The future of the plastic processing industry holds both challenges and opportunities as the industry adapts to changing market dynamics and growing concerns about sustainability. Here are some key aspects that may shape the outlook for the future of the plastic processing industry:

Sustainability and Circular Economy:

There is an increasing emphasis on sustainability and the need to reduce plastic waste. The industry is expected to focus on developing more eco-friendly materials, adopting recycling technologies, and implementing circular economy principles to minimize environmental impact.

Bioplastics and Bio-based Materials:

The demand for bioplastics and bio-based materials is expected to grow as companies and consumers seek alternatives to traditional petroleum-based plastics. These materials offer the potential for reduced carbon footprint and increased biodegradability.

Advanced Manufacturing Technologies:

Additive manufacturing (3D printing) is gaining traction in the plastic processing industry, enabling rapid prototyping, customization, and reduced material waste. The continued development of advanced manufacturing technologies will drive innovation and offer new possibilities in plastic processing.

Industry 4.0 and Digitalization:

The integration of digital technologies, automation, and data analytics (often referred to as Industry 4.0) is expected to transform the plastic processing industry. Smart factories, real-time monitoring, predictive maintenance, and enhanced process control are anticipated to elevate efficiency, productivity, and overall quality.

Regulatory Environment:

Governments and regulatory bodies worldwide are imposing stricter regulations on plastic usage, recycling, and waste management. The industry will need to adapt and comply with evolving regulations, which may lead to innovations in material composition, recycling infrastructure, and waste reduction strategies.

Shift in Consumer Preferences:

Consumers are becoming more conscious of the environmental impact of plastics and are demanding sustainable alternatives. This shift in consumer preferences is driving manufacturers to develop eco-friendly products and packaging, influencing the direction of the plastic processing industry.

Collaboration and Partnerships:

The plastic processing industry is likely to witness increased collaboration between stakeholders, including manufacturers, researchers, governments, and NGOs. Collaborative efforts will drive innovation, address environmental challenges, and develop sustainable solutions.

Chapter 10

Conclusion

In conclusion, "From Melt to Mould" provides a comprehensive guide to the world of plastic processing, covering all the key aspects of the process from melting the plastic to moulding it into the desired shape. This book is an essential resource for anyone interested in plastic processing, including the Entrepreneurs of Plastic processing unit, Startup in Plastics, Machine Operators, Engineers, and Technicians. By following the information and guidance provided in this book, readers will gain a deeper understanding of the plastic processing industry and be well-equipped to achieve success in their operations.

9 789355 549297